GOD'S THEME PARK OF LIFE

C. Clay Westby

INFINITY
PUBLISHING

Copyright © 2010 by C. Clay Westby

ISBN 0-7414-6159-5

Printed in the United States of America

Published October 2010

INFINITY PUBLISHING
1094 New DeHaven Street, Suite 100
West Conshohocken, PA 19428-2713
Toll-free (877) BUY BOOK
Local Phone (610) 941-9999
Fax (610) 941-9959
Info@buybooksontheweb.com
www.buybooksontheweb.com

This book is dedicated to my beautiful wife, Lynn, and my children, Kaila and Craig.

Acknowledgments

Special thanks to my mother, Donna Westby, who assisted me in the editing process.

I would also like to thank family and friends, especially my Aunt Kathy, who previewed this book, and offered helpful comments.

Illustrators for this book were my nephews, Elliot Runciman, age 15 and Levi Runciman, age 12. Robert, their father, drew the rainbow. Their artistic talent is much appreciated.

Contents for

GOD'S THEME PARK OF LIFE
PARK TRAINING MANUAL.

At the beginning of each life lesson there is a rule, or maybe just a thought. At the end of the lessons, there will be quotes for you to ponder.

Preface

With the exception of the work that is quoted or prefaced in some way; this book is based upon my thoughts, experiences, observations, and perceptions. The thing about writing this book is that the words that fill the following pages will get analyzed, critiqued, dissected, and examined. It is a given that some, but certainly not all, the views or opinions contained in this book have previously found their way to ink and paper. If any human error was made regarding anything in this book, please do not hesitate for one moment, to go directly to God, and let Him know that you forgive me!

I am hopeful, that in some way, the words that are between the front and back cover of this book will jump out at you, and affect you in a positive way. By writing this book I developed an individual and personal relationship with God that makes sense to me, and works for me in many ways. I am hopeful, that after you read this book, you will have a basis with which you can develop an individual and personal relationship with God that makes sense to you, and works in your life.

We all have questions about this world, and about our own life. We start with, what is the meaning of life? And we continue with questions like: Why did this, that, or the other thing, happen to me, you, or them?

Before reading this book I would like you to read the following sentences, and fully understand their meanings: THERE IS NO MYSTERY, ABOUT THE FACT THAT

LIFE IS A MYSTERY! GOD IS BEYOND ALL HUMAN UNDERSTANDING AND COMPREHENSION!

Now that you have read, and comprehended both sentences, we can move on.

It is hoped that during the reading of this book, you will interpret things in your own way, believe in God in your own way, praise God in your own way, and love God in your own way. And by doing it your way, you can have a personal meaningful relationship with, OUR GOD.

Before you leave the preface area, I think I better talk to you a little bit about how this book is set up. This book is actually a training manual for all of those individuals who visit God's Theme Park of Life. I thought it best to give everyone the opportunity to read this Park Training Manual, because of all the inherent dangers that are actually a part of this park.

There are 19 lessons to go through, and once a person has completed all of the training, he or she will be better prepared to enter the park. It is in your own best interest to attend all of the classes. Really! Seriously! Whatever you do, do not enter the park by jumping to the last pages of this book! Don't let God hear any integrity, honor, or character warning bells! I guess if you feel that the whole attendance policy is a negative thing, then I should let you know that the positive in all this, is that there are no tests, quizzes, or mandatory assignments in any of the lessons.

Let me guess; you're probably wondering why on earth do you have to read a training manual, before you visit a theme park? Was I right? Well, to answer your question, I need you to start lesson 1, and proceed through lesson 19. While the pages lead you to God's

Theme Park of Life, the words on the pages will transcend into your thoughts. When you enter God's Theme Park of Life you will have your answer, even if you forget your question. Thanks for your cooperation. The park management also thanks you.

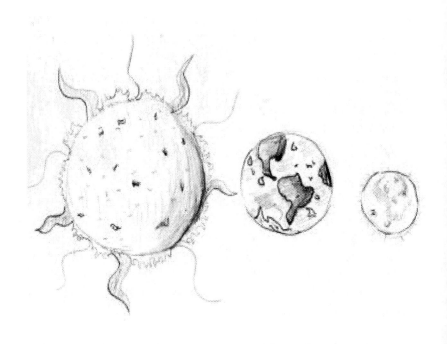

Lesson 1 .... Sun Life

THOUGHT: Sometimes you have to just sit back and take it all in…

Our Planet Earth is a ball of matter that is in constant motion as it rotates around the sun. Out beyond earth is space, and it goes on... and on... and on... We can only assume that space has no beginning, or end.

The sun in our sky creates light for our day. When the sun fades away, and blackness takes its place, our moon is then able to capture the light from the now missing sun. This moon looms above us, along with the stars, providing light amidst all of the darkness. When the sun reappears, another day begins, and time advances one more day.

MORE THAN MANY DAYS HAVE COME AND GONE! In fact earth has existed for, four and a half billion years. Historically speaking; based on our current calendar, and when my book was published, there had been 2,010 years of life on earth pretty much accounted for, and documented, in many different ways. It's just the other 4,499,997,990 years, before our current calendar started, that we have questions about.

We live on earth, and explore what earth has to offer us. We look up, and bend our minds as to the possibilities of what space also has to offer us; not that our minds aren't already twisted in knots from thinking about how we came to be. The solution to earth's beginning may be as easy as evolution.

Christians can accept the theory of evolution, because even evolution has a starting point, and that starting point for me is God. For those of you who have a different theory, or point of view as to how we came to be, it really does not matter, since God is the answer to it all. How we came to be, and how we are allowed to exist, is only by the grace of God.

Very little is known about space and what lies beyond our planet. At this time, it is still unknown if life exists somewhere far away. For reasons unknown to us, life is a part of earth as light is a part of the sun.

The sun keeps our planet alive by providing us with light, and heat. But does the average person ever take the time to even think about the sun, as far as how important it is to our daily lives here on Planet Earth? For most of us, the sun serves only as a reminder that we need to put on our sun-block, and our sunglasses.

The earth, sun, and moon are in constant motion. The earth spins and moves around an average size star that is called the sun. The sun is the closest star to earth. The term closest, which is the opposite of farthest, loses something in the meaning when you stop to realize that the earth is around 93,000,000 miles away from the sun. If you could transport yourself from earth to the sun, and travel at 100 miles per hour, it would take you 100 plus years to reach the great ball of flame.

This ball of fire has a diameter of around 900,000 miles. The earth has a diameter of around 8,000 miles. To put those numbers into perspective; picture the sun as being a gigantic over-inflated beach ball 9 feet in diameter, while the earth would only have a diameter less than a size of a golf ball!

The moon, not being a star, or a planet, is called a moon, because that is what it is, a moon. While Planet Earth moves around the sun, the moon circles the earth.

Before I even started to think about writing this book, I found myself on a hillside near day's end, with random thoughts filling my mind, but yet, still not really thinking about anything; just outside enjoying the day. Looking up, I saw the sun, with all its radiant color, and noticed the outline of the moon beyond the floating white clouds, and the picturesque blue sky. As the wind, or natural forces made the clouds pass by, I pondered about the vastness of it all... and then BAM! It hit me; not like a ton of bricks or anything, but that we are on a spinning ball shaped macrocosm, which continues to travel around the sun, in a perfect life giving way.

Since that one day on the hillside, I look up a lot, you know, taking it all in; everything from the moon and the stars, to Planet Earth and God!

Just clear your mind, take a relaxing breath, and think about the awesomeness of our world!

--- .C.W.

"From now until the end of time, no one else will ever see life with my eyes, and I mean to make the most of my chance."

--- Christopher Morley (2)

"Don't go to the grave with life unused."

--- Bobby Bowden (2)

Lesson 2 .... Life's Start

RULE: Don't be all keyed up thinking about the beginning. At this point, the ending is what matters the most!

God created this specific planet with the ultimate goal of giving people, who were made in His image, a place to experience life. He did it by the POWER OF GOD, and created all things in a matter of a week, or He did it by the POWER OF GOD, and had evolution do the work for Him.

Creationism:

"In the beginning God created the heavens and the earth." On the first day God created "light." On the second day God created the "sky." On the third day God created "land" with "seed bearing plants" and "trees;" He also created the "seas." On day four God created the "sun," the "moon," and the "stars." On day five God said: "Let the waters swarm with fish and other life;" and He also said: "Let the skies be filled with birds of every kind." On day six God said: "Let the earth bring forth every kind of animal;" and "God created people in His own image." On day seven, "God rested from all of His work." "And God blessed the seventh day and declared it holy." ---- Genesis 1$_{(3)}$

7 days! As humans, it is very hard to accept the possibility that God made this world in just six days, and rested on the seventh day. Is it possible that God's time table then, was different than ours is now? In order to even accept that creationism is true, one would have to let go of human logic, and just go on faith alone; and maybe that's what God wants.

Creationism plugs into the seven day work week rather well; which tells me that God likes us to work, but He also wants us to take some time to remember Him. God showed us that on the seventh day He rested, so of course, we should rest one day every week too.

There is nothing in the Bible that states that we have to accept creationism as a fact. It is possible, that someone was just being a creative story teller when they wrote some of the words in Genesis. I mean, it is possible, isn't it?

The following is a very simplistic, evolutionary, narrative time line. The years noted in this paragraph are definitely not exact, but they are not wild crazy guesses either; or are they?

The earth got its start 4.50 billion years ago. Less than a billion years passed by when simple cell organisms popped up. Another half a billion years went by before photosynthesis became a part of the earth. At the 2 billion year mark, complex organisms appeared. After one billion years went by, multi-cellular life, in one form or another, sprang up. Later, simple animals showed up, and just over 500 million years ago there was an onset of complex animals. When 475 million years came about, plants sprouted up on land. Approximately two hundred million years came and went until earth saw the emergence of the dinosaurs. By the time the 150 million year mark rolled around mammals were running around on land, and birds were flapping their wings in the sky. 65 million years ago the dinosaurs ceased to exist! Over sixty million years passed before a species, related to man, was introduced to earth; about 2.50 million years ago. Around 200,000 BC humans, who kind of looked like you and me, arrived on the scene. If God did make our world by way of evolution, it's very apparent that it took a whole lot longer than a week!

Throughout earth's long history there have been many ice ages and volcanic disasters, along with geological movements, and astronomical happenings. After each natural disaster, life ended, life survived, and life evolved. The earth has not stopped evolving, and it continues to evolve today.

Based on fossil evidence, and carbon dating, the theory of evolution is an accepted theory by many. I am very open minded about our whole beginning. For evolution to work for me, it is my opinion, that all of the above natural disasters and events, happened in the order that they did, and the way that they did, so Planet Earth would develop into a living planet; a planet that humans can not only live on, but also rule over. For nature to be so perfect, in the way that everything has unfolded in the past, and is still unfolding, could not be possible; yet, with God, anything is possible. Thank you God! Thank you God! Thank you God!

Possible answers to the start of life: God and evolution, or God and creationism, or possibly, even a little of both!

When you factor in everything unknown to us, but known to God, then you just have to trust in God. God knows how the world was made, and that's good enough for me.

It seems, lately, that a day goes by like a snap of a finger, and Christmas is always just around the corner. Time is one of those things that just keeps on going, and going, and going. So much time has passed by since the beginning of our world that none of us will ever know all of the answers to our past; heck, we probably don't even know all of the questions! There is no debate about the fact, that there was a beginning for Planet Earth, so it stands to reason that there will be an ending. The Bible already has a name for it, it's called Judgment Day. For me, personally, I'm going to leave the past in the past, and get myself lined up and squared away for Judgment Day. Given the choice between heaven and hell, I choose all of eternity in heaven; thank you very much!

So nature; without any prompting from God, just happened to make the right oxygen level, the right climate, the right resources that gave us the means to have an industrial revolution, the right seeds for planting, the right soil for growing things, the right foods to eat, the right water sources, and other miscellaneous resources. And nature also made the earth the right distance from the sun, the moon, and the stars, and made this, that, and the other thing so perfectly... Right!... Sure it did... NOT!!!

--- C.W.

Who is right and who is wrong? In the end, I don't think it will make a bit of difference; there is an end... right?

--- C.W.

Life is a mystery... there, I hope I cleared that up for you!

--- C.W.

"Yesterday is History
Tomorrow is a Mystery
Today is a Gift
That's why they call it
The Present."

--- unknown author

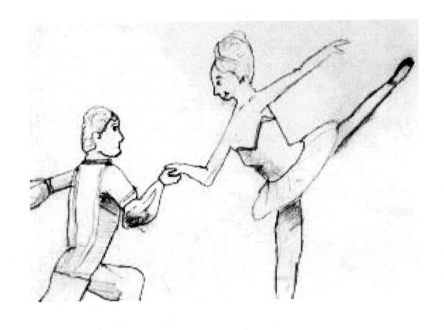

Lesson 3 .... Physical Life

THOUGHT: Supreme Beings are perfect, and human beings are not.

When humans, who resembled modern man, showed their face on earth around 200,000 BC, a cloud of mystery started rolling in. It is possible that man, since the beginning of time, followed the natural course of evolution. God, however, may have stepped in from the project He was already working on, earth, to give man an evolutionary boost. It is also very possible that some time before modern man appeared on the scene, anybody else resembling man, became extinct. Then God simply took man out of the evolutionary equation, and created a modern man and woman in His unique and Godly way.

The actual physical body and brain that make up a human being are beyond magnificent, in and of themselves. The way everything works or functions, and the way the brain and body work collectively together, is truly amazing. Looking at what we are, physically, from the tips of our toes, to the tops of our heads, we find that we are truly an astonishing and unique species. The intangibles about a person are even more spectacular: Thinking and reasoning abilities, thoughts, imagination, and so much more. I am guess-ti-mating here, but there must be a zillion things that make up a human body, so pretty much, unfortunately, a zillion things can go wrong with it too.

The human body and brain, being physical in nature, can get sick with diseases, break down, stop functioning, and die. The causes for these attacks on the human body are genetic, environmental, self inflicted, and random. A lot of the time, there is no rhyme or reason as to why some humans have problems, and other humans do not. Remember, SUPREME BEINGS ARE PERFECT, AND HUMAN BEINGS ARE NOT!

The health of any human can start out bad, and end bad, but it can also start out good, and end good too. Being a still born baby is a bad day for any human being. Dying younger than most, and in pain, is also going to be a bad time for anyone. Making it through that first day alive, and living a long and wonderful life, until a day comes when one dies in their sleep, is what most people at least hope for.

In between the beginning and end of this life and death continuum, there are a great number of human beings, who for one reason or another, have to cope with pain and suffering; some for a short period of time, others for a long period of time, and still others for their entire human life. Human beings can even have physical challenges, or mental challenges. I could go on and on, but I think I have scared myself enough, to the point that I just want to go hide in a corner, and throw a blanket over my head. But then I realize how many people get to enjoy this world, for the most part, with healthy bodies and brains. I mean really, statistically speaking, most people have a brain and body that get through life on earth pretty much unscathed.

When mental or physical problems enter the picture, humans often ask questions such as: "Why did that happen to me, you, us, him, her, or them?" "Why does God make some suffer, and others not suffer?" When Jesus was being treated inhumanely, suffering, and dying on the cross, Jesus uttered the words: "My God, my God, why have you forsaken me?" ---- Matthew 27(3)

God does not pick or choose who suffers, and God had not forgotten about Jesus dying on the cross. God just allows the physical world to exist, without any interference from Him. The physical world starts out with life, and ends in death. What happens in between to a person, either physically or mentally, is just a part of life away from heaven.

Don't blame God if something goes wrong with your spectacular, but imperfect body or brain. He already knows all about them, and all the things that can go wrong with them, because He is the one that gave them to us. God gave us these bodies, because He wanted us to be on earth for only a period of time; so ultimately, we would join Him in heaven where we will all have perfect, spiritual, heavenly bodies. By having imperfect bodies and brains on earth, isn't that a motivator to want to go to heaven?

"What we are born with is God's gift to us." "What we do with it, is our gift to God."

--- anonymous (2)

"Your body is the temple of the Holy Spirit, who lives in you, and was given to you by God."

--- 1Corinthians 6:19 (3)

"Success; it is what you do with what you've got."

--- Woody Hayes (2)

"Make the most of yourself, for that is all there is to you."

--- Emerson (2)

Lesson 4 .... Gift of Life

RULE: Believe in God the Father, God the Son, and God the Holy Spirit. Believe that Jesus died on a cross for our sins, and for the salvation of all mankind!

As was the custom, in biblical times, many different cultures and groups of people sacrificed animals, as a ritualistic act, to appease different God(s). Stated another way; groups of humans sacrificed animals as a plea to their God(s) to forgive them, and to keep them in good favor.

Our God, understanding all, wanted to show us how much He loved us. He wanted to give a special gift to the entire human race; those that lived on earth in the past, the present, and in the future. Our God was going to do something that no other God has ever done, or will ever do; our God was actually going to put us before Himself. God knew that this would only be possible by way of an ultimate sacrifice. This is why God had His son leave His side, and become human for a period of time.

God's son (Jesus) walked the earth as a human being, experiencing life in a physical body. He was able to taste, touch, hear, feel, and see. Jesus, (God) the man, with (God), the Holy Spirit, stayed true to Himself, true to His Father, (God), and true to mankind. He completed the many things that He was sent to earth to do, without committing a sin. He gave us knowledge about God, faith, and spiritual direction.

When the time was right, God implemented His plan to save all human beings from their sins. He did this, when He gave us a Godly gift, and allowed His only son to die on a cross as a human being, for human beings, so all of mankind's past, present, and future sins could be forgiven. Knowing that if He sacrificed His own son, all would know how much He truly loves us. We did not have to find a way to be in our God's everlasting favor and good graces, because God found favor in us. ALL WE HAVE TO DO IS BELIEVE THAT GOD GAVE US THIS GIFT! The "gate" to heaven will be open to anyone that accepts God's gift. (For gift acceptance details, refer to this lesson's rule!)

When the symbolic act of Jesus dying on the cross for our salvation took place, Jesus in His human form, still had to endure all of the pain, wretchedness, and suffering that went with it. Three days after Jesus' human body died on the cross, He ascended into God's Heavenly Kingdom.

Our omnipotent and wonderful God did not have to do any of this; but He did. He especially did not have to have His only son leave His Heavenly Kingdom, to become human, and die a very humiliating human death; but He did. This all powerful God of ours did it, because WE ARE HIS CHILDREN TOO!

"Let your light shine."

--- Matthew 5:16 (2)

Look at death from now on as a good thing, bad thing... Death: a really bad day for the body, but a really good day for the Holy Spirit, because the body turns to dust, and the Spirit gets to return to God!

--- C.W.

You are never alone, because God is always with you!

--- C.W.

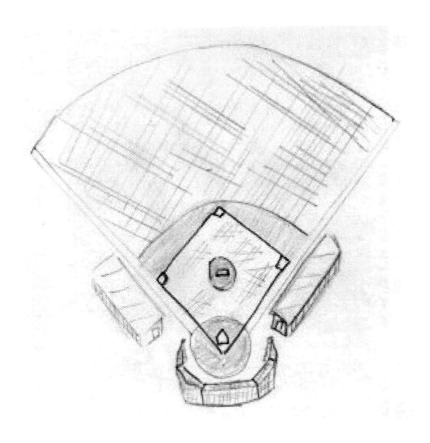

Lesson 5 .... Game of Life

THOUGHT: Some people digest life, and other people just get indigestion!

When God created earth and this physical world, He also made up a game called the Game of Life! Humans are the players that play in this game. Unfortunately, the Game of Life is not played on a fair and equal playing field. If you want any clarification of the game rules, ask God.

I will now give you the most general of general particulars, concerning the Game of Life. Please be aware that this is an incomplete description of the game. I am just trying to give you a quick overview, to make you picture the game, as you are reading along in this lesson. Are you ready? Here we go! Metaphorically speaking, when playing the Game of Life, a ball is what life throws at you. Life can throw curve balls, knuckle balls, fast balls, or even junk balls. And a bat is what is used to hit the balls. You know, hit what ever life throws at you! A person can hit a single, get a strike, or hit a double. One can hit a foul, hit a triple, strike out, or hit a home run. You can apply this game to everything that happens to you in this life. For example: You just get done with a job interview, and you are offered a job; HOME RUN!

The earth is currently populated with about 7,000,000,000 players. Player development starts with genetics and then moves to the environment. Players grow socially, physically, and mentally.

Players can fall victim to random unknown forces, circumstances, and events. These occurrences might influence, disrupt, or even end a player's life. Other happenings can just as easily impact a player's life in positive ways!

I guess we could just say BAD happens to some: bad stuff, bad things, bad life! And GOOD happens to others: good stuff, good things, good Life! Life is not always one or the other. Most players have both good and bad things happen to them in their lives.

I can't remember, have I told you that the players who play in the Game of Life, do not play on a fair and equal playing field? Oh, I did? Oh, that's right, I did! Well then, great, just great. Just wanted to make sure that I did, that's all.

Let's take a look at some of the players who have already played the game.

Player (A) was born into a high society family. He grew up, and was smart, healthy, athletic, good looking, and rich. He led a good life, and he had a good life on earth. He died in his sleep at age 75.

Player (B) was a beautiful woman, full of life and energy. She was 21, and the whole world was in front of her. She was one of those rare individuals, who are aware of how lucky they are. For this reason, the young woman spent time volunteering at an area hospital. She spent her volunteer time sitting and talking with children less fortunate than herself. One rainy and windy night she left the hospital and started for home, but on her way home she fell asleep, and she lost control of her car. The car crashed into a tree, and her human body died.

Player (C) was an entertainer of sort. He grew up and led a wild, chaotic, exotic life. He was rich, and had a fun filled life. He died at age 85 of natural causes, and his wife, who was a 27 year old Victoria Secret model, came to his funeral to pay her respects.

Player (D) was born poor, and lived a poor life. He got sick, and didn't have enough money to buy any medicines. He died at age 48.

Player (E) was just an average person. He had a wonderful family, a good job, and treated people nicely. One day he was driving home from work, and a drunk driver crossed over the center line, and crashed into his car. This average man survived, but spent the rest of his life in a wheel chair.

Player (F) was a little girl, about 2 years old, when a relative committed a sex act against her. The sex offense, kept on being repeated over and over again during the passing years. When the child turned 9 years old, she told her parents about how she had been raped by her uncle. Her parents reported the matter to the police, and the uncle was arrested. When the girl was 17 years old, she committed suicide.

Player (G) was an average teenage girl. All of her girlfriends kept telling her about their sexual experiences. None of her friends were using any protection, and they had been having sex with multiple partners. At age 15 the girl fell in love with a boy, and at age 16 she decided to have sex with him. The sexual experience was an emotional experience for the girl. It became more than an emotional experience, because from that one act, and one sexual partner, she contracted Aids. At age 26, her health deteriorated, and she died.

Player (H) was a child that was born with a genetic defect. The child spent most of his life in and out of hospitals. He died at age 12.

There is no guessing at this; life on earth is good for some, and bad for others. Life on earth is even great for some, yet it is terrible for others. In fact, LIFE ON EARTH IS MARVELOUS, WONDERFUL, AND FANTASTIC for a lot of people, but DEVASTING, PAINFUL, AND BRUTAL FOR OTHER PEOPLE.

If a rich man clings to God, because of all the blessings that he believes that God gives to him, and a poor man clings to God for hope and inspiration; upon their death, it is assumed that each of their souls would rise up and go through the gates of heaven for all eternity.

If a rich man calls his life blessed, what does a poor man call his life?

Some people have everything they ever wanted in this physical life, while others do not have anything. Why does God allow some people to have such a good life on earth, and others to have such a bad life? The answer is simple: ONLY GOD KNOWS.

I believe that since the Holy Spirit lives in all of us, God loves everyone the same. Remember, God shares all of our feelings, and emotions; which include all of our pains, sufferings, joys, and triumphs.

God created this physical world for humans. Just for a minute, I would like you to think about yourself; you being a human, and all. I mean, really think about who you are physically, socially, and mentally. Think about all that you have been, all that you are, and all the person that you hope to be. Now take the time to think about others in that same way. By doing this mental exercise, you will probably come to the same conclusion that I have: HUMANS ARE AN AMAZING SPECIES, AND GOD MADE US, SO HOW TRULY MAGNIFICENT GOD MUST BE!

I know I'm testing your patience, but I would now like you to think about earth. Think about all the land masses, the waterways, different forms of life, the air we breathe, the water we drink, the food we consume, and all of earth's natural beauty. Then if that isn't enough for you to ponder, think about all the other things on earth life here has to offer you. After thinking about earth for a bit, you will probably realize that this planet is a wonderful place for humans to live. EARTH IS AN AMAZING PLANET, AND GOD MADE IT, SO HOW TRULY PERFECT HEAVEN MUST BE!

God allows the human race, and the planet that we live on, to be; for lack of a better word, HUMANLY. Humans can be: Good, bad, healthy, unhealthy, happy, depressed, lucky, unlucky, rich, poor, smart, dumb, common, uncommon, neat, messy, loud, quiet, fun, dull, pretty, ugly, mean, nice, athletic, not athletic, short, tall, weak, strong, and the list could go on and on. HUMANS ARE WHAT THEY ARE, AND THE PLANET IS WHAT IT IS!

To keep everything in perspective, while we are here on earth, one only has to remember that our physical life is not a Godly life, and it is very much finite. Earth is a place where you have to accept the good with the bad, and so on, and so forth. SO BASICALLY, WE ARE AMAZING, BUT, YET, IMPERFECT BEINGS, LIVING IN AN AMAZING, BUT, YET, IMPERFECT WORLD!

Spiritual life in heaven is infinite, and heaven is pure, loving, beautiful, and perfect. God, in all His wisdom, made an imperfect world that is nothing like heaven, because He wanted to make sure that all of His children would seek Him out. God made an imperfect world; isn't that a motivator to make us want to go to heaven?

Well, since we have already talked about the Game of Life a little, there should be nothing wrong with looking at the game in a competitive way. Bearing in mind all of the rules etc. found in the Bible, it makes no sense to any competitor, that there is only one chance to play in this game that we call life. From a competitor's stand point, it would even be okay if there was only one try at the Game of Life, if at the start of it, all the way to the end of it, all things were equal; health, riches, intellect, long life, etc. It would then be human against human, all competing to get into heaven, on an equal and level playing field.

To repeat myself: The Game of Life is not fair, and this everyone knows! Reflecting back to the day that I was born, which is not that easy you know, well anyway, I vaguely remember popping out and hearing a distant whistle. And then I am pretty sure that I heard God yell… "PLAY BALL!!!"

Don't do tobacco, alcohol, or other drugs, because they can sideline you from the Game of Life!

--- C.W.

If life was a cake...
You would have certain people thinking that life is a cakewalk.
Others would say that life is a piece of cake.
Some would get a bite of cake here and there.
Then there would be those, who only get the cake crumbs, and that is pretty crumby, no matter how you slice the cake!

--- C.W.

Is there a reason for us to be here? Heaven is perfect and infinite, and earth is imperfect and finite; I mean, why not just go directly to heaven?

--- C.W.

When is life ever simple? Short answer: It's not!

--- C.W.

"God has not promised us a quiet journey; only a safe arrival."

--- unknown (2)

Lesson 6 ....Cycle of Life

THOUGHT: This may be another gift from God; it's just wrapped differently.

It could be debated that by having His son leave heaven to walk on earth, and then return back to Him, God may have indicated that reincarnation, in some form or another, exists. Human bodies live, and human bodies die, but the Holy Spirit, and/or soul lives on!

When trying to figure out this world, some people connect with God by looking at life as a cycle. When you think about life, not being fair and all, a cycle of life, of some type, can help make sense of it all.

The following is theory, or speculation; oh what the heck, I'll throw in the word conjecture too, as to how the reincarnation process might work. Please keep in mind that the standard ONE LIFE, ONE BODY, ONE SOUL, WITH ONE RESURRECTION VOUCHER, is still at the top of the list, when it comes to plausible religious salvation systems.

God, who is all things, and the beginning of everything, allows Holy Spirits, which are a part of Him, to experience earth in human vessels. God too, gets to experience human life through this reincarnation process. Even though, we as humans are not Gods, we are Godly in the sense that the Holy Spirit lives in us, and is a part of us.

God, who is holy, pure, and good, had a Holy Spirit break away from Him to be his own entity away from God. When this Holy Spirit chose a life without God there was only one direction for him to go, because when he left all that was good, the only path for him to take was all that was bad and evil. This first spirit to leave God, who is still present today, is known as Satan. Satan is the ruler of hell, and all that is evil.

A Holy Spirit experiences a physical life on earth by way of a human body, and is intertwined with a man's conscience. When the vessel, or physical body in which the Spirit resides, passes away, the Holy Spirit returns to God; to once again continue its spiritual life in heaven.

If a Holy Spirit, or conscience of a man, gets caught up in Satan's grasp, this Holy Spirit, upon the death of the physical body, would go to a place that is between heaven and hell; some call this purgatory.

If a Holy Spirit, or conscience of a man, becomes numb to God for one reason or another, upon the death of the physical body, the Holy Spirit would go to hell where Satan rules.

All Holy Spirits that exist in heaven, purgatory, or hell will get to experience life on earth an unknown number of times. All Holy Spirits start each experience here on earth when they re-appear during the beginning stages of another human being's life cycle.

Luckily, God is all about love and forgiveness! Even those Holy Spirits who have flirted with the dark side have the opportunity to return to God!

If a Holy Spirit turns completely away from God, and bad replaces all that is good, then the soul is no longer Godly; it is now only evil. This transformation happened with Satan. Presently, we see this from time to time, when a sociopathic killer pops up. It is common that we refer to a sociopathic killer as a person without a conscience. These souls have already chosen an eternity in hell.

We know that humans are prone to sin, but it is possible that a person's conscience, with the help of the Holy Spirit, can be developed to the point that a person can move mountains! Although it is possible, it is not very probable, because, well, after all, we are human!

By now, you are probably doing a lot of thinking about whether or not reincarnation is a possibility, and you most certainly have some questions about it. Here are some common questions and answers.

How does this whole reincarnation thing actually work? Answer: ONLY GOD KNOWS!

Does a spirit just jump into a body without knowing anything about it? Answer: ONLY GOD KNOWS!

Does a Holy Spirit have to leave heaven? Answer: ONLY GOD KNOWS!

Really, seriously, does reincarnation even exist? Answer: ONLY GOD KNOWS!

It does not matter how many questions I write down, and for that matter, you can even add some questions to my list, because all of the answers will be the same: ONLY GOD KNOWS!

Yes, answering questions about reincarnation, or about God in general, is as simple as that!

He, that is all knowing, is God, and he, that isn't all knowing, is man. If God wanted us to know everything, He would have made us Gods, not humans.

The next logical question is: Will there ever be a time when God enlightens us at all, regarding any of our questions? Answer: ONLY GOD KNOWS!

Oh, I almost forgot, before we close the door on this lesson, I should go ahead and tell you that memory loss is also a part of the whole reincarnation process.

That is why, what happens in heaven, stays in heaven, and what happens in our prior lives here on earth, stays with our prior lives!

End of Theory_____

If you want my personal take on the whole thing, I would have to tell you that it is okay to believe that life on earth is a cycle; which it might be, but then again it might not be, so be ready either way!

"The greatest evil that can befall a man is that he should come to think evil of himself."

--- Goethe (2)

"There is nothing the body suffers which the soul may not profit by."

--- George Meredith (2)

"Four things can not come back: The spoken word, the spent arrow, the past life, and a neglected opportunity."

--- Arabian Proverb (2)

Lesson 7......... Life of the # 7

RULE: When in doubt pick # 7.

By way of the Bible; God, or things related to God, are associated with the number 7. God picked out only one number, and uses that specific number, to get us to REMEMBER HIM!

If you spend any time reading the Bible, and you come across the number 7 in any form, i.e., 7, 27, 77 etc., the first thing that should pop into your head is God! It stands to reason, that if you come across the number 7, even when you are not reading the Bible, God will still pop into your head for a second or two; and that is exactly what God had in mind.

Numbers have always been, and are still very much, an important part of our life. It only makes sense that God would want to have a presence in our number system, as well as in our words.

The # 7, in and of itself, has no power, because it is only a number. The power comes when you see the number 7, and you instantly think of God.

As the number 7 is associated with God, the number 6 is associated with Satan.

Let's have some number fun, with the number 7... 7 times.

1.) Mathematically speaking, 7 is a stronger number than 6, because the number 7 is a prime number!

2.) In mathematical terms, the number 7 has power over the number 6, since the number 7 is a bigger number.

3.) 7 minus 6 = 1, and there is only one God.

4.) 7 plus 6 = 13, and the number (13) can represent the conflict between good and evil.

5.) 7 rhymes with heaven!

6.) There are 7 things expressed in the Lord's Prayer; really! Look for yourself.

7.) A rainbow has 7 colors.

7 QUOTES

"The shortest and surest way to live with honor in the world is to be, in reality, what we appear to be."

                                        --- Socrates (2)

"Things turn out best for those who make the best of the way things turn out."

                                        --- Art Linkletter (2)

"Courage means being afraid to do something, but still doing it."

                                        --- Knute Rockne (2)

"Every moment of your life, including this one, is a fresh start."

                                        --- unknown (2)

"Whatever one believes to be true either is true or becomes true in one's mind."

                                        --- John C. Lilly (2)

"The universe is change; our life is what our thoughts make it."

                                --- Marcus Aurelius Antoninus (2)

"I have prepared for death all my life, by the way I lived."

                                        --- Socrates (2)

Lesson 8 .... Prayer Life

RULE: Spend at least 1 minute a day praying to God,
praising God, thanking God, or just talking to God.

A lot of people have the whole prayer thing customized, and individualized to the point that their prayers are more like shopping lists of individual wants and needs.

Instead of praying to God the way we want to, let us pray to God the way He would like us to pray to Him. Let us put God before ourselves! Do you remember when He put us before Himself?

BY WAY OF THE LORD'S PRAYER, JESUS SHOWED ALL OF US HOW TO PRAY!

God already knows what your individual wants and needs are. You do not need to pray for what God already knows. And God doesn't just want to hear from us when we are up to bat and the bases are loaded, and all He can hear is: "Please God, please God, please let me hit this ball over the fence; please, please, please!" Although spontaneous conversations with God are well and good, one should take the time to really THINK ABOUT GOD, THANK GOD, and PRAISE GOD.

When the things people pray for happen, do you think it is the power of prayer, a flip of a coin, a chance happening, or a coincidence? Let me give you a hypothetical example that in real life has undoubtedly happened. Variations of this example, with different circumstances, happen a lot in this world!

Two Christian families both had a sick family member in the hospital. Both were children, who were expected to die. The two children shared the same hospital room and had the same medical problem. Family members of each child gathered in the same room each day, being separated by only a curtain. One hospital bed on one side of the curtain, and one hospital bed on the other side of the curtain. One day all of the family members for both kids were in the room, standing in their respective areas. Each family began to pray that their loved one's sickness would pass and that their son, daughter, brother, sister, grand-daughter, grand-son, be allowed to live. After a day or two had passed since the two prayer meetings, medical personnel told one set of parents, that their child was going to be okay. The parents who received the good news along with other relatives walked into the above hospital room, and paraded around showing signs of joy, happiness, and relief. One of the family members, for whatever reason, pulled away the curtain that was still separating the two sides of the hospital room. When the curtain was pulled back it revealed that no one was on the other side of the room. The second bed, where the other child had been, was still there, but the child was conspicuously missing. During the night, this child had died.

If any prayer works out for someone; is it an answered prayer, or is it just life unfolding in its natural unbiased way? In the mind of the person doing the praying, I am sure he or she perceives it as being an answered prayer.

Since God wants us to pray a specific way, I am leaning towards the assumption that God does not take any prayer requests. And yes, I am aware that miracles do happen, which neither science nor man can explain. About that, I would say, OUR GOD is an all powerful God, so I am not ruling out the possibility that God, at times, exercises His right to bless anyone, or any situation, at any time.

The Bible contains the Lord's Prayer, which shows all of us how to pray to our God.

This is a common version of the Lord's Prayer. JESUS ACTUALLY SPOKE THESE WORDS:

"Our Father, who art in heaven,

Hallowed be thy name.

Thy Kingdom come,

Thy will be done, on earth as it is in heaven.

Give us this day our daily bread.

And forgive us our trespasses, as we forgive those who trespass against us.

And lead us not into temptation, but deliver us from Evil."

The "Give us this day our daily bread" line, definitely gives us all a big hint, that this prayer should be said everyday.

Keep in mind this is not an individual grocery list type prayer. When you say the Lord's Prayer, you are saying words like (WE) and (US). This prayer has people praising God, forgiving each other, and praying for one another. The power of one prayer.................... AWESOME!

A good way to make this prayer meaningful to you, and more personal between you and God, is to begin the Lord's Prayer by making the sign of the cross. When making the sign of the cross you can focus on God the Father, God the Son, and God the Holy Spirit. By doing this you will make God's words live in your mind, in your heart, and in your soul.

The following can be done silently, or out loud; reader's choice!

(Move one hand up, and lightly touch your finger tips to your forehead.) Say: "God the Father," then say: "Let me be mindful of you."

(The finger tips of the same hand are now placed over your heart, and are actually touching your chest.) Say: "God the Son," then say: "Let me think about your human heart beating, while you were dying on the cross for me."

(The same hand now moves to one shoulder, and then to the other shoulder.) Say: "God the Holy Spirit," then say: "Let me be aware that you are a part of me."

After this salutation, continue your prayer time with God, by saying the Lord's Prayer.

The following is my interpretation of the Lord's Prayer.

1.) Our God in heaven,

2.) We (the human race) honor you, and your name.

3.) At any time, let your Heavenly Kingdom come upon us (the human race).

4.) Let your will be done on earth as it is in heaven.

5.) Please give us (the human race) what we (the human race) need this day.

6.) Forgive us (the human race) for our sins, as we (the human race) forgive those who commit sins against us (the human race).

7.) Do not let us (the human race) stray from your will, and keep us (the human race) from thinking bad thoughts, and doing bad things. Protect us (the human race) from all that is evil.

I know that the average person is kept busy, day after day, with, you guessed it; day to day things. Not that I timed it or anything, but the Lord's Prayer can be respectfully, and meaningfully delivered to God in about one minute. Even on your busiest day, take one minute to focus on God, and on the rest of God's children, which of course, includes you.

You are probably wondering if God would be okay with a relationship that only lasts sixty seconds a day? Yes!! Of course He would.

"Timing has a lot to do with the outcome of the rain dance."

--- unknown author (2)

"Prayer never seems to work for me on the golf course. I think it has something to do with my being a terrible putter."

--- Rev. Billy Graham (2)

When talking about the American Civil War, Abraham Lincoln once said: "We, on our side are praying for victory, because we believe we are right; but those on the other side pray to Him too, for victory, believing they are right. What must He think of us?"

--- (2)

Lesson 9 ..... Rainbow of Life

RULE: Enjoy this life, and play nicely with others!

Let's just say that at one time God was not pleased with all the violence, and probably some other things that He saw in the world, so He kind of opened up a faucet, and flooded the earth.

"Then God told Noah and his sons, I am making a covenant with you and your descendents... " "I solemnly promise never to send another flood to kill all living creatures and destroy the earth." "I am giving you a sign as evidence of my eternal covenant with you and all living creatures." "I have placed my rainbow in the clouds." "It is the sign of my permanent promise to you and to all earth." "When I send clouds over the earth the rainbow will be seen in the clouds, and I will remember My covenant with you and with everything that lives." "Never again will there be a flood that will destroy all life." "When I see the rainbow in the clouds, I will remember the eternal covenant between God and every living creature on earth." "Then God said to Noah," "Yes, this is the sign of my covenant with all the creatures of the earth." ------- Genesis 8 (3)

The rainbow can be seen all over the world! I'm pretty sure everyone has seen a rainbow, but a rainbow is just a rainbow, unless you know exactly what a rainbow is! Yes, there is the scientific definition of course, but getting past all of the scientific jargon, a rainbow is a visual reminder of a promise that God made to all of us. The promise that God made, is a PROMISE OF LIFE! Now that you know about the promise, I hope you look at a rainbow from now on, while keeping that in mind.

Since the promise was for the entire human race, it makes perfect sense that God would give us a rainbow to symbolize all the many colors that make up the human race.

When you are looking up at the next rainbow that you see, and you are thinking about God, these are the 7 shades of colors that you might see: red, orange, yellow, green, blue, indigo, and violet.

Wouldn't it be cool if every time a person saw a rainbow, whether the person was alone, with a group of people, at a stadium filled with people, with a friend, spouse, neighbor, or stranger, the person, and everyone else present would just pause for a few seconds, and praise God!

"The greatest joy one can have is doing something for someone else, without any thought of getting something in return."

--- John Wooden (2)

"I shall pass through the world but once. Any good therefore that I can show to another human being, let me do it now."

--- Mahatma Gandhi (2)

"You can never do a kindness too soon, because you never know how soon it will be too late."

--- Ralph Waldo Emerson (2)

"The smallest good deed is better than the best intention."

--- unknown (2)

"I always seek the good that is in people and leave the bad to Him who made mankind and knows how to round off the corners."

--- Goethe (2)

Lesson 10 .... Purpose of Life

THOUGHT: The purpose of life; is life itself.

God gave all of us a purpose way back when!

"Male and Female He created them." "God blessed them and told them," "Multiply and fill the Earth... " ------ - Genesis 1 (3)

When you are married, and you don't have any kids, you can say my purpose in life, but when you have kids, it is mandated somewhere, that MY gets changed to OUR.

My wife was my purpose in life, but when our kids showed up on the scene, they became our purpose in life.

To clarify things a little bit more, what I should have said was that my wife is still MY purpose in life, but our kids are OUR purpose in life. It is the same purpose, but only much bigger.

Let's back up a little bit, just like they do in the movies.

My wife and I fell in love, and my purpose in life was pretty simple; all I had to do was be a good husband to her. We wanted kids someday, but we first wanted to make sure that we had a solid relationship before we had them. One of the things we learned early on, is that a simple touch went a long way in making both of us feel good about each other, and about our relationship.

Intimate touching is important in any marriage. In fact intimate touching is at the top of my list! But wait, could there be different types of touching that are just as important to a marriage? On any given day my wife and I hold hands. Sometimes we give each other spontaneous quick little kisses and hugs. At times, we just have a hand, arm, or leg touching each other while we are sitting on the couch, or when we are sleeping in bed. It's not like we play twister on the couch and in bed or anything, but we just end up touching each other a lot. And yes, all of the other ways that we touch each other are just as important as the intimate touching, because any touch sends the message of trust and love, and those two words should be a part of any marriage.

Anyway, let's get back to the plot of things. Our relationship grew, our love grew, and then my wife's belly grew, and grew, and grew... and then poof! Our first child was born... and then we yelled: "WE ARE PARENTS... YES!!!!" After the initial celebration, I looked at my wife, and my wife looked at me, and then we looked at our baby in her arms, and we both screamed: "WE ARE PARENTS?!!"

My purpose in life went from simple, to not so simple. I started to think about the fact that my wife and I were now responsible for another life! Another baby life!!

Later on, not that same day or anything, we had our second child, and my purpose in life, oops; I mean OUR purpose in life, got even bigger!

I don't care if you tell, yell, scream, or shout at a new couple about how their lives will change when they have kids; they will not fully comprehend any of it, until they too are called "Ma Ma" and "Da Da."

MARRIAGE IS INSTANT PURPOSE, HAVING A FAMILY IS A GODLY PURPOSE!

There are additional purposes in life besides marriage and family. I mean, one does not have to be married, or have a family, to have purpose. I think God gave us some automatic purposes to life, because he did not want to see anyone standing around idly.

59

The purpose IN life, OF life, or TO life, can be anything you love to do, and have a passion for doing; as long as you are willing to share whatever it is you like to do with God. It can be things like golfing, cooking, bird watching, hiking, reading, fishing, hunting, going to work, having a hobby, playing or watching sports, anything and everything can be purposeful. The purpose of this life is to have purpose in this life, or in most cases, purposes!

If you keep an eye to heaven when you are living this life, you will add purpose to your life; which, as it turns out, is the single most important purpose of them all! This purpose is to live life, with the life goal of being in the next life; which is… an eternal life with God!

"A hug is a great gift. One size fits all and it's easy to exchange."

--- unknown (2)

"To be trusted is a greater compliment than to be loved."

--- George MacDonald (2)

"Make yourself necessary to somebody."

--- Ralph Waldo Emerson (2)

It is hard for us to envision eternity. Days end, months end, years end, but ETERNAL EXISTENCE...... Never Ends!!

--- C.W.

Lesson 11 .... Words of Life

RULE: Keep God's words alive!

The Bible was put together by collecting way more, than A LOT, of probably written documents, letters, stories, books, and other miscellaneous writings. The Bible was actually put together by humans. Bravo for the human race; we actually did a good thing. But humans, through no fault of their own are, well, human! When we think back to when people were working on the Bible for a very, very, very… long time, it is pretty darn easy for any of us to assume that some of the material was intentionally left out of the Bible, accidentally left out of the Bible, or just left out for one reason or another. During the process of making the Bible words had to be interpreted, translated, and rewritten. It is possible that mistakes were made, either accidentally, or on purpose, and words could have also been intentionally deleted, or added to existing texts. After the original Bible was made the words again had to be interpreted, translated, and re-written into different languages. I am not trying to imply that the Bible was put together incorrectly in any way. What I'm trying to convey is that God did not write the Bible; He inspired others to write the Bible.

What did I just say? I said: THE BIBLE WAS WRITTEN BY MAN; INSPIRED BY GOD.

Though there were countless verbal and written testimonies, scrolls, papers, stories, documents, pictures, books, and other writings present when the pages to the Bible were compiled, not all of it was used; which means there is probably still enough left over material somewhere, that could still be used to make a Bible 2… Bible 3… Bible 4… etc. Obviously, no one was thinking of a Hollywood deal when this thing was being planned out; I guess they had more Godly interests in mind.

Biblical scholars, now and in the past, with faith at their sides, hold the Bible up, and announce the Bible to be the work of God. THE BIBLE... GOD'S WORDS! The Bible has withstood the test of time, and if anything, the words in the Bible are growing more and more powerful each day. I encourage one and all to read the Bible with an open mind, an open heart, and with the awareness that the Holy Spirit is a part of you.

The Bible holds the living words of God. The words in the Bible show us how much God loves all of us. As long as people keep reading the Bible, talking about the Bible, interpreting the Bible, either correctly or incorrectly, discussing topics in the Bible or even debating things that are in the Bible, God's words will stay alive. As long as these things happen God will not be forgotten, and God will be pleased.

If we were to mention one of those debated topics, I guess we could talk about baptism. You know; the whole wash away your sins ritual. To wash, or not to wash? That is the question. Well, we know that Jesus was baptized, so that bit of information has to be pretty good for the people on the one side of the topic. People on the other side, are quick to point out that baptism is not a mandatory thing for entering heaven. Mandatory, or non-mandatory? That is the new question. Well, since there is nothing wrong with doing a little extra credit, I think a better question to ask is: When and where can I wash?!! And just so everyone is in the loop regarding this topic, baptism in general, is when water is symbolically used to wash away your sins; as opposed to you jumping in a lake with a bar of soap!

GOD'S COMMANDMENTS ------- Exodus 20 (3)

God made it very clear that He wanted us to obey all of His commandments. If it was important enough for Him to say the words, and have them put in the Bible, then I guess they are important enough for me to put them in my book.

GOD SPOKE THESE WORDS:

1.) "Do not worship any other God besides Me." My interpretation - Love God.

2.) "Do not make idols of any kind." My interpretation - Do not bow down or worship anything, or anybody, except God.

3.) "Do not misuse the name of the Lord your God." My interpretation - Only say God's name in respectful ways.

4.) "Remember to observe the Sabbath day by keeping it holy." My interpretation – Church for some, rest for others, but honoring God, should be for everyone. You can honor God daily by saying the Lord's Prayer.

5.) "Honor your father and mother." My interpretation - Always be respectful of your parents.

6.) "Do not murder." My interpretation - Do not kill anyone.

7.) "Do not commit adultery." My interpretation - Do not "cheat" on your spouse, or "cheat" with another person's spouse.

8.) "Do not steal." My interpretation - Do not take things that don't belong to you.

9.) "Do not testify falsely against your neighbor." My interpretation - Do not lie.

10.) "Do not covet your neighbor's house." My interpretation - Do not be jealous of anything that someone else might have.

Did you know if you spend about 15 minutes a day reading the Bible, you could finish reading the Bible in the same amount of time that it takes the earth to make one lap around the sun? Just FYI, it takes approximately 365 days for the earth to circle the sun one time. Well, if you are not interested in racing the earth around the sun, simply put your Bible out somewhere in your house, and read the Bible whenever you want, for as long as you want. God is probably okay if you just look at the cover of the Bible when you are coming and going, because when you look at the cover, you think about God, and that works for Him! God just doesn't want to be forgotten.

The Bible has been around for generations, and generations, and generations, and generations, but in the Bible ------- Matthew 4$_{(3)}$ it says: "The Kingdom of Heaven is near.".... define NEAR!... When trying to interpret the word NEAR I guess it could still mean time, but wonder if it was talking about distance? Wonder if it means heaven is close to us right now?

--- C.W.

"Many people are bothered by those passages in the scripture which they cannot understand; but as for me, I always noticed that the passages in scripture which trouble me the most are those I do understand."

--- Mark Twain $_{(2)}$

Lesson 12 The Life of a Super Hero

RULE: Just say NO!

The Super Power of saying NO! It's not the coolest type of power as far as all the powers that are given out in the Super Hero community; nevertheless, it's a great power to have!

We have the power to say NO! The power to say NO, can keep the NO Super Hero physically and mentally strong. This power is so great, that by using it, a person can even CONTROL a situation that could be harmful to them physically, mentally, and socially. Other Super Heroes have never been given a power like this; this power is unique only to humans. Can you name a Super Hero that has this power?... I can name one:_____ (You!)

This power can be used in many situations. When asked to chew tobacco, you have the power to say NO. When asked to smoke a cigarette, you have the power to say NO. When asked to drink beer or other alcohol, you have the power to say NO. When asked to have sex when you really don't want to, you have the power to say NO. When thinking about committing a crime by yourself, or if you are asked to commit a crime with some friends, you have the power to say NO. When asked to smoke marijuana, you have the power to say NO. When asked to take a harder drug, you have the power to say NO. When you are thinking about cheating at something, you have the power to say NO. The list goes on and on. This power can be used for virtually everything that comes across your path in this life.

You only have to use the power of saying NO when you, the Super Hero, are facing dangers. All Super Heroes have senses that alert them to when danger is close by, or even when it is somewhere out in the distance. The important thing is to not work against your Super Power. When your senses pick up danger, and they warn you mentally that this, that, or the other thing is not going to be good for you, in one way or the other, then don't question your Super Power; act on it by saying NO. Having this Super Power comes with great responsibility when trying to protect yourself from the evils in this world.

At times you might be face to face with danger and need an instant NO. Other times you will be able to say NO ahead of time, so you don't put yourself in a bad situation. Just believe in your Super Hero Power. Always use it, and everything will be fine.

Oh, one more cool thing. All NO Super Heroes can put their NO response on automatic pilot. This protects them if something in life jumps up, and surprises them so much, that their Super Hero senses are not able to give them a clear alert signal. When this happens, the automatic pilot drops a NO bomb instantly. By having a built in automatic "NO" response, a Super Hero is protected immediately; which will give any Super Hero time enough to evaluate everything. If, after a few seconds, minutes, hours, or days, it is found that the surprise was a good thing, as opposed to being a bad thing, then the Super Hero can go ahead and throw away the NO, and say yes. Please do not worry about wasting a NO here or there; you have an unlimited supply of them, because, after all, you are a Super Hero.

If you fail to use this Super Power in a given situation, it could lead to negative consequences for you, and your life. It could cripple you mentally, physically, and socially; and that would not be good for any Super Hero.

If you ever give up your Super Hero Power, and say yes to alcohol, tobacco, and other drugs; these things can have power over you. At one point you will want to say NO, but your mind, and your body will work against you. ADDICTION IS REAL! HEALTH RISKS ARE REAL! SELF IMPOSED UGLINESS!!

MAY YOUR SUPER POWER ALWAYS BE WITH YOU!!!!

"Three daily reminders: Have the courage to say no. Have the courage to face the truth. Have the courage to do the right thing, because it is right."

--- W. Clement Stone (2)

Lesson 13......Life's Choices

RULE: Life is not to be understood, but lived.

One of the best ways to live your earthly life is to always try to do the right thing. I mean really, after all, wouldn't that be the right thing to do?

It is true that anything and everything can happen to us at any time; some of it good, some of it bad, some of it really good, and some of it really bad, but that's life! One can spend their whole life trying to understand life. It just may be that LIFE IS NOT TO BE UNDERSTOOD, BUT LIVED, and to live it the best way we can. One does not have to understand this life to live this life!

God has given humans free will, so living life means making choices, and the choices we make will ultimately define the person that we are, or the person that we will become. With that being said, God asks all of us to follow His will on earth as we would in heaven. He gives us free will, yet He wants us to use our free will to follow His will, if we are willing to do that. I guess I will leave that one up to you, because after all, you do have a free will!

In any given evil situation in which we find ourselves, we should walk away from it, and follow in the footsteps of Jesus. Since we are humans, it is possible for us to walk away from any situation, but not so possible to walk in Jesus' footsteps. However, if you do come up against any evil encounter, or situation, and at the end of it you know in your mind, in your heart, and in your soul that you did the right thing; then I'm quite positive you will find your own path to heaven.

If, by free choice, you choose to do drugs and drunkenness, be prepared to stop living life, and to start living each day for that drug; be it cigarettes, alcohol, marijuana, or other drugs.

God just wants us to enjoy this earthly life as much as possible, while still maintaining a God approved life style. As humans, let us try our best, and let God take care of the rest.

To recap what has already been said: God in His amazing wisdom allows all humans to be unique in their own individual ways. He does this by giving us free choice in everything we do; good luck with that!

"There is a choice you have to make in everything you do. And you must always keep in mind that the choice you make, makes you."

--- anonymous (2)

"Choose your friends carefully. If you hang with dogs you'll end up with fleas."

--- unknown (2)

"Take pride in yourself. Be your own person. Don't do things because everyone else does them. Don't be a part of the crowd. Dare to be different. Never be afraid to stand up for what you believe to be right, even when it means standing alone."

--- Jack Lambert (2)

"Never undertake anything that you would not have the courage to ask the blessing of heaven."

--- Georg Christian Lichtenberg (2)

Lesson 14 ...... Life with Faith

RULE: Think about God.

Faith verses knowledge: It's apparent, that while on earth, God is only going to allow us to have one of them; so faith is what we cling to. It stands to reason that all Holy Spirits in heaven can let go of their faith, and just live KNOWINGLY, in God's Heavenly Kingdom. KNOWINGLY; wouldn't that be something?

Even though faith is a workable system in a religious setting, I still think that it would be cool if God would just open up the sky, present Himself to us, and tell us exactly how to live the kind of life that He wants us to live.

If God were to open up the sky and show Himself to us, the meeting would probably go something like this: We would see our God above the clouds. Some human would yell: "Give us direction;" "Give us the rules to live the kind of life that you want us to live." God would reply by saying: "I ALREADY DID!!" "DID YOU NOT GET YOUR COPY OF THE BIBLE?" Then the sky would return to normal.

If that meeting did take place, and God did not verbally go over the details of living a good life, the way I figure it, it still would have been a win - win situation. We have the Bible, like we have always had, and the face to face meeting with God would have increased everyone's faith in God exponentially!

There are blinking thoughts that go away in a blink of an eye, surface thoughts that go away as quickly as they come, and then there are deep thoughts that linger to help increase one's focus. Any way that you have the opportunity to think of God is a good way! I will let you in on a secret that you probably already know. If you are spending any time at all, thinking about God, then your faith in God is present and accounted for.

If you want to increase your faith in God, spend some time concentrating on God, and on the relationship that you have with Him. Reading the Bible, and praying also help in the process of acquiring more faith, but it is the mental strength that will make your faith strong. You know the kind of strength I'm referring to, the kind when you're able to FOCUS ON GOD FIRST, AND THIS EARTHLY LIFE SECOND!

"The spirit and faith that we possess inside each of us is what really matters."

--- Socrates (2)

"I do not want merely to possess faith; I want a faith that possesses me."

--- Charles Kingsley (2)

"Faith dares the soul to go further than we can see."

--- William Clark (2)

"Security is not the absence of danger; it is the presence of God."

--- unknown (2)

"The Lord is my strength, of whom should I be afraid?"

--- Psalm 27:1 (2)

"The greatness of our fear shows the littleness of our faith."

--- anonymous (2)

Lesson 15 ...... Life In...Worry Out

RULE: Pull God in, and push worry and lack of control out!

Today, should we worry about our lack of control, or try to control what we worry about?

People should not worry about what they don't have control over, because they are not going to be able to live life if they are too busy worrying about it. Just so everybody knows, and no one is left in the dark; people do not have control over anything! God has control over everything!

I guess, in some ways, human beings do have a little control over what they eat and drink, think, say and do. We shuffle these things into the self-control category.

IN QUESTIONABLE MATTERS, THE HIGHEST LEVEL OF SELF-CONTROL OCCURS WHEN A PERSON THINKS AND THEN LISTENS TO THE HOLY SPIRIT, BEFORE SAYING OR DOING ANYTHING.

What do we know so far? We know that on a personal level we have hardly any control over our lives. And guess what? We can't control other people, or what happens to them either! We have no control regarding what happens to us, or around us. Basically, we have gone from having no control, to having some control, and now we are back to having no control; is that about right?

Some worrywart type thoughts can even consume you. They eat at you, and eat at you, until you are mentally spent, and exhausted. When you think about it, some thoughts can be so thoughtless!

Let's be mindful of the fact that the mind can work for you, as well as work against you. I'm not a psychologist or anything, but I bet if you were to make an appointment to see one, the psychologist would tell you the same thing. On a Christian level, if you are focusing on God, I mean really focusing your thoughts on God, how would you ever have any "thought space" left over for any lack of control, or worry problems? And focusing on God can be done anywhere and everywhere, without an appointment!

Fact # 1: For the most part, no one has control over anyone or anything. No one, not me, not you, not anyone, not them, not her, not him, not us, not anybody, no where, no way, no how, nobody, no one... well... no one EXCEPT for God, that is.

If fact # 1 is a fact, and I am sure that it is, because it is listed as a fact, and a fact is a fact; why would anyone worry about what they can never have control over, which appears to be everything?

Factually speaking, control issues and worry issues should no longer be your issues. If you are a person that tends to worry, and attempts to control things, then I guess if anything, you should be upset at the fact that it is useless and meaningless to worry about anything, because you don't have control over anything; in fact you only have control over nothing. Hey, wait a second! Wait a darn second here. What did I just say? Did I just say something about nothing? I think, I said something about actually having control over something, which is nothing. Oh! Wow! The mud has been wiped away, and things are now crystal clear. It is a glorious day for all worriers and controllers, because now it has been brought out in the open! There is finally something that worriers can worry about, and have control over, and that something is NOTHING!!!

If you are a worrier, you now have a choice! You can either worry about anything, or you can worry about nothing. For those of you, who choose to worry about nothing, refer to the framed pictures at the beginning of this lesson. There you will actually get to see pictures of what nothing looks like!

It is hoped that worriers will not add extra worry to their day, by worrying about how silly it is to worry about nothing. Because when you think about it, worrying about anything is just as silly! Still, if you like a busy day, worrying will surely keep you occupied. If you decided that you wanted to free up your time, to live the way that God wants you to live life, just throw all of your "ANYTHINGS" and "NOTHINGS" to God.

"Can all your worries add a single moment to your life? Of course not."

--- Mathew 6:27[3]

"Worry is a futile thing, it's somewhat like a rocking chair; although it keeps you occupied, it doesn't get you anywhere."

--- anonymous [2]

"Good morning! This is God. I will be handling all of your problems today, and I will not need your help. Just stay close to Me and enjoy your day."

--- unknown

Lesson 16 .... Church Life

RULE: Love and respect your neighbors.

At one time, all humans spoke the same language. "The Lord confused the people by giving them many languages thus scattering them across the earth." ------- Genesis 11(3)

I'm just ball parking it here; but I'm guessing that God did not want us all to be the same.

God wanted people to have different languages, and different cultures. And guess what? That's exactly what He got. Worked out pretty darn good for Him I would say.

When God populated the world, and separated the human race, it is only logical that different cultures would have different religions, which, in my opinion, can, in one way or another, lead to our one God.

He did not want one world religion; He wanted many religions reaching out to Him and praising His name in different ways!

Its funny, those born into one religion or the other, will probably stay in that religion, and I'm thinking God is fine with that. Some people might not agree with me, and I'm fine with that!

All the different religions give people a base, from which to reach God. Each religion allows for some separation of beliefs, ideas, and doctrines. A given religion may have different branches, churches, divisions, subdivisions, organizations, and groups. A person belonging to any one religion can even have an individual, personal belief system. I'm not so sure God wanted there to be so much separation within the same religion, but hey, if all religions can lead to God, then I guess it follows suit that all of the many ways of worshiping Him, within a given religion, can lead to God too!

Well, this much we know: In the world there are numerous people, different cultures, different languages, and different religions.

There are 7 billion people spread out all over the world in North America, Asia, Africa, Europe, South America, and other places.

The languages spoken are: Chinese, English, Spanish, Hindi, Arabic, Russian, Bengali, Portuguese, Japanese, German, French, and others.

The religions all over the world are: Christianity, Islam, Hinduism, Judaism, Buddhism, Chinese Folk Religion, and others.

We are all God's children, so let us all be good neighbors and love each other! The good neighbor policy states that we should respect each other's culture, religion, and language. And since we all live in the same neighborhood called earth, it would be a very good thing if we didn't judge each other! That way we can be respectfully free, to shout out, and praise God, in the way that works for each one of us!

Let's just say that Christianity, or the Christian religion is the right religion for you. Not that it should be, or even would be, but just that it could be! If being active in this religion, or any other religion is important to you, then you will need to decide on how, and where to worship God. The cool thing for Christians right now is that there are a number of churches all honoring God in their own way.

A church is a very special place, because of what it represents. It represents a "House of God." If someone asked me what my definition of church would be, I would simply say: COMMUNITY, INTERACTION, DOCTRINE, AND A HOUSE IN WHICH TO PRAISE GOD.

God likes that whole love thy neighbor thing, and that love and neighbor thing fits a church like a glove. A church is a great place to meet your neighbors. A neighbor is not just the person who lives next door to you. A neighbor, in the biblical sense of the word, means the human race; so good luck planning a dinner party for all of your neighbors!

The good thing about there being so many churches is that it's kind of like being in an ice-cream shop with all the variety of ice-creams to choose from. I mean, you don't have to buy the first scoop of ice-cream that you see; just like you don't have to join the first church that you come across.

You can even take several taste tests until you find the ice-cream that you love. As far as churches go, you can go in a church, out of a church, in a church, and out of a church; there are no rules to church testing.

With napkin in hand, you pick the ice-cream that does it for you. In your mind it is the best tasting ice-cream; delicious!

It's done; you have picked out a church that is the right church for you. You feel comfortable with the church leaders, the church doctrine, and the people who attend the church. It's a match made in heaven, so to speak.

No church has ever had control over you, or will ever have control over you, so go ahead and become a member of any church in which you would like to get involved. Churches give us memberships, but God gives us the gifts of LIFE and SALVATION. HAVE A MEMBERSHIP IN A CHURCH, BUT FAITH IN GOD!

"If I were ever prosecuted for my religion, I truly hope there would be enough evidence to convict me."

--- John Wooden (2)

"Not always right in all men's eyes, but faithful to the light within."

--- Oliver Wendell Holmes (2)

"To believe in something and not live it, is dishonest."

--- Ghandi (2)

"I am just a common man that is true to his beliefs."

--- John Wooden (2)

We are the same in really only one way; we are all humans. We are different in so many ways, because we are human. Let us celebrate the fact that we are all human beings, and respect each of our many differences.

--- C.W.

"I looked for God in all the temples, mosques, and churches, and found Him in my heart."   ---unknown

STONEHENGE

Lesson 17 .... Societal Life

RULE: View all current societies as changing in an ultra-slow, continual, and positive progression. That way you can accept the world's present societies the way they are, as opposed to the way you want them to be.

I'm sure all over the world there are people in each given society saying things like: "Our society is really messed up." People who say things like that, obviously, do not adhere to the rule in this training lesson.

To continue the training, we will just go ahead and pick on the United States. It appears that some people have been complaining about various problems in this society. Here is a list of things that some of the American people are, shall we say, commenting negatively on: education, healthcare, the economy, unemployment, and the criminal justice system.

The above list is a bit overwhelming, but to be fair to the United States, the lists for the other societies in this world are just as long. To have people gain a new perspective on things, so they can view their own society, and/or all of the societies in the world in a positive way, we only have to give them a glimpse of the past; then have them participate in a small training exercise.

Two of the first ancient civilizations were Mesopotamia, and Ancient Egypt. They got their start around 3000 BC, but things came to an end for both of them between 600 BC, and 25 BC. Those two ancient societies lasted well over 2,000 years. After the above two societies ended, there were others to take their place. From the first societies, to the present day societies, there have been thousands of years of ultra-slow, continual, and positive progression. The U.S.A. came about in 1776 AD and this book came about in 2010 AD. There are only 234 years that separate 1776 from 2010; which means, this country has a long way to go, and grow, before it reaches the 1000 year mark!

In general, the U.S. society and other current societies today are still plodding along in an ultra-slow, continual, and positive progression! Well, lately, the whole technology thing has been experiencing a growth spurt, which at this time definitely makes it an exception to the "plodding along" idea!

Now that we have had a brief look at the past, the training exercise can begin. It starts when participants mentally take a trip backwards through time and envision themselves, as being non-royals, living in one of the ancient civilizations. The trainees have an up close, mental awakening when they look at the politics, power, culture, religion, science, technology, and the people that made up the first societies.

After the participants come back from the short trip, they are asked only one question: "Do you want to live in your present society, or would you rather go back in time, if it was possible, which it is not, and live in one of the first societies?"

The responses have always been pretty much the same. They say things like: "No matter how messed up our present day society is, we will take here and now, instead of then and there!"

During the retrospective training session, the trainees were never told how any of the modern day societal problems could be fixed. But maybe, just maybe, the trainees will now, at least, be able to put on rose colored, new perspective eye glasses, and see the problems in our society as being only WORKS IN PROGRESS!

Societies have only been around for approximately 5,000 years. In comparison to the age of the earth, societies have only existed for a very short period of time. You can say that again!! In comparison to the age of the earth, societies have only existed for a very short period of time; which of course, leaves room for lots of improvements!

From time to time it is good to look back into the past, because the past is our beginning, and without a past, there is no beginning, and that would not be good for any of us. The past should not be forgotten, or dismissed. The ability to write, and document history was very much present in Ancient Egypt and Mesopotamia. Learned things were, and continue to be, passed on from one generation to the next. We should respect all those who have come before us, because they have made our world a better place to live.

There have been numerous historical events recorded in one way or another. One particular event deeply impacted the world! That event was the life and death of Jesus Christ, Our Lord and Savior.

Wow! Christ's life impacted the world so much that even the calendar system was adapted to separate old world history, BC, with new world history, AD, and the birth of Jesus was the dividing line. BC stands for "Before Christ," and AD stands for "Anno Domini; which means in the year of the Lord." The intent to divide the periods was there, but the dividing line was just a tad off, because later it was learned that Jesus was born around "4-6 BC," and died around "33 AD." Nevertheless God's mark; "AD" was left on the world's calendar for everyone to see. Question: "What year was this book published?" Answer: "2010 AD." There He goes again; not wanting to be forgotten! (1)

The United States of America is so new, that it is still working out all of the kinks... obviously!

--- C.W.

"Individual commitment to a group effort – that is what makes a team work, a company work, a society work, and civilization work."

--- Vince Lombardi (2)

"Most things that were once believed impossible are now common place."

--- unknown (2)

"You must be the change that you wish to see in the world."

--- Ghandi (2)

Society punishes people when they break criminal laws... it's called jail. We punish ourselves regarding moral laws... it's called guilt.

--- C.W.

Human ingenuity; reach God any way that you can!

--- C.W.

Lesson 18 .... Life on the Big Screen

RULE: What happens on the big screen should stay on the big screen.

Hollywood has desensitized the human race regarding violence, drugs, alcohol, cigarettes, cigars, swearing, saying God's name in disrespectful ways, and crimes. The amount of influence that a given show has on its viewers is tremendous. When kids and adults see movie stars smoking, doing drugs, drinking alcohol, committing crimes, saying God's name in disrespectful ways, swearing, and acting violent, it is bound to influence them in negative ways.

Watching shows produced by Hollywood, or other sources, is a free choice thing. If you find yourself watching a show, that your great, great, grandmother would probably not approve of, then follow this rule: WHAT HAPPENS ON THE BIG SCREEN, SHOULD STAY ON THE BIG SCREEN. Be the person that you think you should be, not the person Hollywood attempts to influence you to be!

From time to time, Hollywood does produce some very uplifting, and positive movies.

The following movie was done right! I would even feel good about inviting and buying movie tickets to this show for God, and His Son. Heck, I would even spring for the popcorn too, if sometime in the future They take me up on my offer!

I would really like it, if you the reader, would watch this movie. I encourage you to watch this movie. Watch it, talk about it, and think about it.

The envelope please... drum roll... envelope opening up... the name of the movie is... "FACING THE GIANTS"... standing ovation!

Just for the fun of it, I want to tell you about a game that is for kids, but adults can play too. It is called, for lack of a better name, "The Reading Game." It starts when players who have a book in their hands are in front of the TV, and the TV is turned on; sounds pretty good so far, right? In fact, a player can turn the channel to his or her very favorite show; it could even be cartoons. As soon as the first commercial comes on the screen, the players have to mute the commercial and jump into their books. They have to remain reading until they see the actual TV show back on the screen. If people play this game a lot they will get to watch TV, and improve their reading skills; it's a win-win situation! I bet there will be more than a few occasions, when the mute button will be left on, even when the show pops back up on the screen. Want to bet? (Every hour of TV has about 15 minutes of commercial time.)

Be more concerned with your own character, than the characters you watch in the movies or on television. Remember, God is watching LIFE all day long, and you are one of LIFE'S characters!

--- C.W.

"We need people who influence their peers and who cannot be detoured from their convictions by peers who do not have the courage to have any convictions."

--- Joe Paterno[2]

"Character is what you are in the dark."

--- Dwight L. Moody[2]

Lesson 19 ....The Flow of Life

RULE: Stay on course!

If a natural water source is un-interrupted, the flow of water is constant, and can usually be seen running down its natural path. For a human being, the flow of life is much deeper than any waterway, and is anything but constant as it follows many courses.

When water hits a rock, or other objects, its path is altered. Given time it usually seeks out and finds its original natural path. When people hit a bump in the road of life, their life may be altered or adjusted, yet, they are usually pretty good about getting back on course again. Most of the time, people are able to just go with the flow of things during their day to day lives, and are not really affected by much. They don't let the little things in life bug them. They just, "Go with the flow."

A person's course in life is somewhat complicated so we will keep it simple, and say that any course is a good course for a person, if that person wants to be on that course! Humans don't seek in one direction like water does; humans live life in a multi-directional way. Humans don't usually run up against actual rock-like walls that make them turn one way, or the other. With people, everything and everybody can impact a person's life, which may, or may not, affect whether or not a person stays on a given course. Some people end up taking a hard course, and doing things the hard way, while other people end up taking an easy course, and doing things the easy way. The course a person follows depends on a lot of things: preparation, proper planning, the right time, the right place; then there is dumb luck, and just how the ball bounces.

If water hits a giant boulder, it may take some time, but eventually the water will again find its natural path. If people hit a BIG bump in life, and they are thrown way off course, then it might take a period of time for them to get back to the life they want to have. The person who hits a BIG bump will not automatically flow back to their intended path or course like water does. A person will have to come up with a plan of action to get back on course again. Friends and family are always a plus, but each individual person has to depend on, and look out for, himself or herself when planning a course of action.

Now you know! The natural flow of water is definitely a drop or two different than the flow of human life!

Most people like the flow of things in their life, and they don't want it to be interrupted by any type of a bump. If people like how things are flowing, and they like all the courses that that they have been on, are currently on, and will be on in the future, why would any of them voluntarily get themselves lost in this life? You know, steer themselves off course, to the point where they may never be able to find their way back to the life that they could have had, would have had, or should have had. Yet some do; some people actually choose to lose their way, so to speak, and they do this by smoking cigarettes, chewing tobacco, drinking excessive alcohol, taking other drugs, committing crimes, and doing miscellaneous other things. Any of these, can cause a BIG bump in life, but more than that, they can be LIFE STOPPERS!!!

But it's only tobacco! Tell that to the smoker who is currently in the hospital, and will never be able to have the full life that he or she could have had, would have had, or should have had!

Some people who get involved with LIFE STOPPERS lose their way right away, while others become lost over a period of time!

I have talked to jail inmates about this subject. When I sat down and talked with them, they just seemed like regular Joes. I asked each inmate the same question. I asked: "How did you mess up your life so badly?" They all pretty much said the same thing: "Drugs and alcohol."

Before we continue with the rest of this lesson, I should tell you, that there is quite a big difference between just being a "little bit lost," and the kind of "lost," where you are never able to find your way back.

Being a little bit lost will not land a person in jail or in the hospital. Being a little bit lost, is not being the person that you want to be, or going down a course or path you don't want to be going down. The person who is a little bit lost is not living their best life.

Remember, in general, God gives us life, along with the ability to steer ourselves onto better courses. That way you can be all you want to be, and more importantly, all God wants you to be.

Instead of being like a leaf, just floating down the stream of life, I hope you choose to be like a salmon that forges their way up-stream.

The path in life for each person is never the same; some paths are easy, and some are quite hard, but stay your course as best you can. You will always find your way back, using God as your compass. Poor life, rich life, average life; just don't make it a lost life!

"It is a very bad thing to become accustomed to good luck."

------- Publilius Syrus (2)

"Let us throw off everything that hinders and the sin that so easily entangles, and let us run with perseverance the race marked out for us."

------- Hebrews 12:1(2)

5 P'S: "Proper Planning Prevents Poor Performance."

------- unknown

"If it is to be, it is up to me."

------- Frosty Westering (2)

THE EXCITEMENT MUST BE BUILDING UP BY NOW, BEING THAT THIS WAS THE VERY LAST LESSON BEFORE GOING INTO GOD'S THEME PARK OF LIFE! I MEAN, YOU ARE SO CLOSE TO ENTERING THE THEME PARK, YOU CAN PROBABLY SMELL THE COTTON CANDY!!

SO, LIKE, WHAT ARE YOU STILL DOING HERE? GO ALREADY; SKEDADDLE!!!!! GET THESE PAGES A TURNING, AND GET YOURSELF INTO GOD'S THEME PARK OF LIFE AS SOON AS POSSIBLE; NOW IS BETTER THAN LATER. GO! GO! GO!

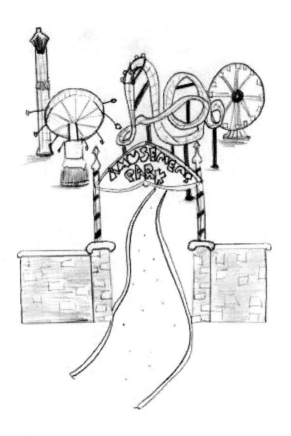

I think I know what you are thinking! I'm thinking, that you are thinking, that this is a picture of God's Theme Park of Life. And if you are thinking, what I'm thinking, that you are thinking, then you shouldn't be thinking that, because this is only a picture of a typical, common, run of the mill, ordinary, amusement park. I guess in some way, this amusement park is kind of related to God's Theme Park of Life, but not really related; kind of a distant cousin type of a thing. But even looking at this picture, will most likely bring back wonderful memories of going on rides and eating cotton candy!

Well, since you are mentally in the wrong park, work your way to the nearest exit. Along the way be thinking that if this pictured park is typical, common, run of the mill, and ordinary, then God's Theme Park of Life must be atypical, un-common, completely unique, and extraordinary in every way imaginable.

When you exit this park by turning the page, you will find yourself at the Grand Entrance to God's Theme Park of Life! Prepare to be amazed! Are you ready?... Get set... Go!

EXIT →

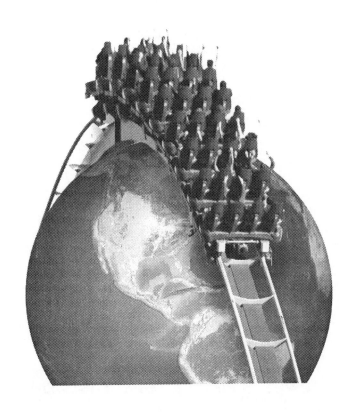

**WELCOME TO PLANET EARTH,
OR WHAT I LIKE TO CALL
GOD'S THEME PARK OF LIFE!**

Keep your hands in, and your seatbelts buckled, because as crazy as it is, the entire human race is on one big ride! Just kidding! Not about the ride, but about having to keep your hands in and your seatbelts on.

God's Theme Park of Life is such a big park that anything and everything can happen.

There are thrill rides, exciting rides, emotional rides, and the list of rides goes on and on. Everything you DO, TASTE, TOUCH, HEAR, SMELL, AND SEE, are considered rides in this park.

Take trips down raging rivers, snorkel in tropical waters, hike in the beautiful outdoors listening to the wildlife as you go, taste foods from around the world, touch your spouse in loving ways, listen to the sounds of the ocean, smell the fragrance of orange blossoms, and watch a thousand sunsets.

While you are in the park, there is really only one rule.

RULE: IF YOU START TO DO SOMETHING, WHEN YOU KNOW IT IS WRONG, THEN IT IS A SIN; SO DON'T DO IT!

Stated yet, another way: IF YOU HAVE AN INKLING OF A THOUGHT THAT YOU SHOUDN'T GO ON A CERTAIN RIDE, THEN DON'T GO ON IT!

ANY SINNING DONE IN THE PARK WILL BE NOTED BY THE OWNER OF THE ESTABLISHMENT.

Since this is God's Theme Park, let's respect the one rule.

Other than the one rule, HAVE THE TIME OF YOUR LIFE, BECAUSE IT IS YOUR LIFE!

Oh, one more thing I should mention; before the park closes, you are encouraged to go on the most amazing ride ever. The ride is called "The Leap of Faith," not to be confused with another ride called "The Leap of Fun."

"The Leap of Fun" is when a person jumps out of a plane. "The Leap of Faith" is when a person jumps into waiting hands.

"The Leap of Fun" is an exciting, adrenalin charged ride, and it begins when the side door to the airplane, that a rider is in, opens up, and the wind starts whirling around inside of the aircraft. The leaper steps to the open doorway, swaying back and forth in a nervous, excited, and animated type manner. The leaper leans forward, and lets go of whatever they were hanging onto, and… ahhhhhhhhhhh!!!!!!!!!

The person is now free falling towards the ground; the rip cord is pulled, the chute opens up perfectly, and the person gives a sigh of relief. The subject lands safely on the ground, and the ride is over.

The ride was a blast! The only complaint the rider had was that sometime during the free fall experience, a wallet and a set of keys were lost.

When people talk about this ride, they say things like: "It scared me to death." "My life flashed before my eyes." "It scared the life right out of me."

A person is now standing in line, waiting for their turn to go on "The Leap of Faith!" The person has time to reflect back on their life. Some of it was good, some of it was bad, but for the most part it was fine. As the line gets shorter the person stops thinking about their own life, and starts thinking about a life with God. It is now the person's turn to go. The subject starts feeling excited, and then the adrenalin kicks in. The leaper leans forward, and lets go of whatever they were holding onto, and... ... nothing! No screaming, no fear of crashing to the ground, nothing, because as soon as the person took the "Leap of Faith" the subject landed instantaneously into God's hands! One thing that happened was a comforting feeling came over the person, a sense of inner peace. The leaper also gave a sigh of relief, like a big burden was lifted from their shoulders. The rider knew that everything was now going to be okay, because no matter what, God was always going to be there. Unlike most rides, this ride never ends!

The person on this ride also had a couple of things fall off. In fact everyone on this ride always has the same things fall from them too. There are two things actually. One is worry, and one is control issues, you know, those things that we can't control. Faith replaces them both.

When people talk about the "The Leap of Faith" they say things like: "This ride is life changing." "This ride is everlasting." "It's the best ride in the park!!"

"The Leap of Faith" also known as "Take the Leap," is open 24 hours a day, 7 days a week, and this book is a free pass to the front of the line. When you are ready, close your eyes, or don't close your eyes. Let go of whatever you are hanging onto, give it all to God, and then............ "TAKE THE LEAP!!"

What I'm kind of hoping for right now is that you will take some time to allow your mind to really absorb all of the many things that were in this book. Think of your mind as a sponge..............or not! Really put some thought into what you got out of the lessons, and how the "park pages" reminded you of the fact, that since your birth, you have always been in GOD'S THEME PARK OF LIFE!

Please feel free to review the lessons and quotes in this book. ENJOY THE TIME YOU HAVE IN THE PARK!

GOD BLESS

References

[1] Gotquestions.org

[2] 1001 Motivational Messages and Quotes, by Bruce Eamon Brown, © 2001 Coaches Choice.

[3] New Living Translation Bible, © 1996 Tyndale House Publishers Inc.

[**] Wikipedia The Free Encyclopedia; http//en.wikipedia.org and other internet websites were used to collect facts and figures for this book.

To my friend Brian

A Note About Me: The Author.

I was born, baptized, and raised as a Catholic. I consider myself to be a bench player in the Catholic Church, but I am an active player regarding my faith in God.

I am a Washington State University alumnus. Once a school teacher, but for the last 20 years I have been employed as a Deputy Sheriff. My family and I reside in Washington State. Being a first time author is quite exciting, and I found this avenue to be a great forum to express my views and thoughts regarding life and God.

C. Clay Welty

360-878-2291